Desert - The Promised Land

Numbers; Deuteronomy; Joshua 1-4

Introduction to the Books of Numbers and Joshua

The people of Israel spent many, many years in the desert, trying to find the promised land. They began by wanting to do all the things God had told them to. But as time went by, they stopped trying and gave up "Who cares?" they said to each other and again they did bad things.

The Book of Numbers describes what happened during the long years in the desert. Numbers could be called "The Complaint Book," because it tells story after story of how the people of Israel would not trust God to take care of them. Instead they grumbled and were afraid.

Again and again Moses begged God to forgive them. God did, but He also punished them by making them wait forty years before He led them to their new home.

Before Moses died, he called his special friend Joshua and blessed him. He told Joshua to be brave and strong. Then Moses put his hand on Joshua, and God passed on to Joshua some of the ways of leadership which had made the people want to follow Moses. Now the people would do what Joshua told them. Joshua was their new leader.

After Moses died, the people were very sad. There had never been a servant of God like Moses. He was the only man to ever talk face-to-face with God. Some of the people knew Moses was a great leader and they prayed God would make Joshua the same.

The Book of Joshua tells all about the wars God's people had to fight in order to win their land of Canaan. This is the story of one of the greatest generals ever, Joshua. But Joshua's greatness was not due to his own cleverness. Joshua listened to God and did what the Lord told him.

IN SEARCH OF
THE LAND
OF MILK
AND HONEY
Life in the Desert

Numbers 9:15-23; 10:11-36

God had a very special way of showing the people of Israel when they should break camp and move on and when they should stay in one place. If they wanted to know, they would look over at God's tent. Whenever God wanted the people to stop traveling and rest in one place, His cloud stayed over the special tent.

The cloud was a sign that God was with the camp. It rested just above the tent. As long as it stayed there, the people of Israel stayed where they were. But if the people woke up one morning and saw the cloud had moved and was waiting for them in the desert, they would pack up all their pots and tents, load everything onto the camels and donkeys and set off after the cloud.

All the people could see the Lord's cloud. Even the smallest child way in the back only had to look up, and he or she would see the cloud and know where to go.

During the two years when the people were camped at Sinai, they learned from Moses how

to follow all God's rules. Day after day passed and weeks became months. Every morning the people looked at the special tent to see if the cloud had moved. They wanted to go to the promised land, but God had not told them to travel yet. So they waited. While they waited, they grew strong and excited about the coming trip. They knew they were going to a very special place.

Finally, two years after they left Egypt, there came a day when the cloud had moved out toward the desert.

"Today's the day!" the people called to each other. It was time to go. Family by family, they all set out. The first ones to leave the camp and lead the people were the priests, who carried the ark, or box, containing the tablets with God's laws written on them.

The ark was the most precious thing the people of Israel owned. Those large stones inside were the proof that they were God's chosen people. There Moses had written down God's rules and promises for them.

After the ark came all the families. It was a huge crowd of people and animals. What a sight! There was so much dust! The nation of Israel was finally on its way to the promised land.

"It All Tastes the Same"

Numbers 11:1-9

No sooner had the people been traveling in the wilderness when they forgot how much they had wanted to travel. They started to complain. Their long rest at the camp by Mount Sinai made no difference. They did not like traveling. They did not like the dust and the unsettled feeling. They did not like walking all day. They did not like living in tents.

Worst of all, though, they wanted meat. The quail God gave them during the beginning of the trip was all gone. Now their only food was the manna bread from heaven. They picked it up every day, ground it up and made little cakes from it.

The problem was not that they were hungry. No, the people of Israel had plenty to eat. The people complained because they were tired of eating the same thing day after day after day, for breakfast, lunch and dinner.

"We're sick of manna!" they cried out.

"If we have to eat another manna cake, we'll die!" they grumbled. They were not at all thankful to have the food. All they could do was complain.

When God heard all the grumbling and saw no one saying thank you for their food anymore, He grew angry. His anger overflowed into a fire on the edges of the camp. The people screamed. Smoke was everywhere. Many tents were burned down in God's anger.

But still, the people did not learn to be thankful for what they had. "Give us meat!" they yelled at Moses.

"We would rather be slaves in Egypt," they said. "At least there we had fresh fish and fruit and vegetables."

"We want our cucumbers!"

"And we want onions and garlic!"

"We want meat!" The people all cried out.

The Meaty Lesson

Numbers 11:10-35

That the people of Israel would have forgotten so soon that God had promised to take care of them drove Moses crazy with frustration. "Are these people like little babies who cannot learn?" he asked God. "Why am I the one who is stuck with these spoiled children?" Moses felt very tired and very old. He did not even like the people of Israel anymore.

Time and time again they had broken promises and given up, without even trying. Now they were making such a fuss about their food, not even realizing they were blessed to be alive and free. God was angry with them, too. But God knew the people's grumbling was not Moses' fault.

Because God did not want Moses to get hurt by carrying the heavy burden of a weak people, He said, "Moses, choose seventy leaders from the people of Israel. Bring them to the special tent and I will send My Holy Spirit into them, just as He is in you. Then the Holy Spirit will help these men. They can do things for you and you will not feel so tired of the people. You will have helpers."

But God was still angry at the people for saying they would have been better off in Egypt. Why, they did not even remember what it was like to be slaves. They had complained then, too. The people were very bad again.

God told Moses He would teach the people of Israel a lesson. "I will send them meat. But I will send them more meat than they know what to do with. And they will grow so sick of it they will never cry out for meat again," God said.

It happened just that way, too. God sent a huge flock of quail to settle on both sides of the camp. The people spent days gathering all the birds. And they ate and ate and ate until they all had stomach aches. Then they ate some more. Many became very sick. God taught the people an important lesson. They should not have complained when they already had enough.

Moses Is Challenged by His Two Best Friends

Numbers 12:1-16

Moses had two very good friends. They were his brother Aaron, who had helped him lead the people out of Egypt, and his sister Miriam, who had watched over him so well when he was just a baby.

Although both Aaron and Miriam had cared for Moses, as the trip through the desert wore on, they felt jealous of Moses' leadership. They, too, had been close to God at times, and they wondered why Moses always got to be the leader. "Why can't we lead the people of Israel sometimes?" they asked themselves.

God heard Aaron and Miriam being mean to Moses. God was not happy. Moses was a good man, a very good man. He did not care

about being the leader. Over and over again he had asked God to please take the leadership away from him. Moses never did feel he was the right man for the job. He and God were like best friends. God did not want anyone saying bad things about Moses.

God called Aaron and Miriam to come with Moses to the special tent. The cloud came down over the tent and God told Aaron and Miriam how they should not be jealous of Moses. Then, when the cloud lifted off the tent, Miriam had a terrible surprise.

She looked down at her hands and oh no! Her skin was all white and flaky. She was very, very sick. This was God's way of punishing her for having been so mean.

Aaron cried out, "No, please don't do this to Miriam!"

Moses did not want to see his sister sick either. He called to God, "Please heal her. Please do not make her this way." God listened to Moses, but said Miriam must stay sick and live apart from the people for a week.

When a week was over, God healed Miriam and she was able to come back and join the camp again. From then on, Miriam and Aaron never plotted against Moses. They knew he was God's choice for a leader and they tried their hardest to help him every way they could.

ON THE BORDER
Within Sight of
the Promised Land

Numbers 13:1-30

As the people traveled in the wilderness there came a day when God said to Moses, "Send spies into the country I am planning to give you. Have them see what sort of land it is and what the people are like who live there."

Moses did as God asked. He chose one man from each of the twelve tribes of Israel. These tribes were related to Joseph and his eleven brothers, the sons of Jacob. The twelve men left the camp and the people of Israel waited for them.

After many, many days the men returned. One was Caleb, from the tribe of Judah, and another was Joshua, whom God had blessed as a general. Caleb and Joshua told Moses, "Oh yes! You should see the land. It is so beautiful, with strong trees, and gentle hills. Flowers bloom everywhere and the crops of the people there were rich and plentiful. It really is as God promised, a land of milk and honey."

There was only one problem, though. The people who lived on the land were all very good fighters. Joshua and Caleb knew that with God's blessing, they could drive those people out of the land. Joshua remembered how God had given them victory the time Moses held his hands high in the air.

Not everybody agreed with Joshua and Caleb, though. Some of the other spies were troublemakers. In the end, they spoiled the trip for almost every one of the people of Israel there that day.

"We Are Not Strong Enough"

Numbers 13:31-14:12; Deuteronomy 1:19-33

The other men who had spied out the land with Joshua and Caleb were not so sure the people living in the promised land could be defeated. They were afraid, and they were troublemakers. They lied to the people.

"Oh no, you would never want to live there," they said. "It is a terrible land, the sort of place where you would always be hungry and thirsty and no matter how hard you worked, crops would never grow. Besides, the people living there are like giants and we would just be grasshoppers."

The Israelites believed these other men. They could have believed God's promises, but instead they believed these men who were not brave. "Oh, Moses!" they cried, "what have you done to us?"

Moses groaned. The people were complaining again!

"Moses, we want to go back to Egypt!"

"Moses, we don't want our wives and children to be taken prisoner by these tribes who are stronger than we are. We would be better off as slaves."

"Moses, it was all your idea to leave Egypt in the first place. We should never have listened to you. Look, now we will all die and for what? For a terrible land where no one wants to live anyway!"

Moses, Aaron, Joshua and Caleb fell to their knees. They begged the people to be reasonable and remember the promises of God. But the people would not listen. They were very stubborn and liked feeling sorry for themselves. They were so upset with Moses, they threatened to throw rocks at him and hurt him.

The Lord said to Moses, "What is wrong with these people that again they do not believe Me? I cannot put up with them much longer. They are terrible. I will destroy them and keep you alive and we will start over again."

The Forty-year Punishment

Numbers 14:13-45; Deuteronomy 1:34-46

When Moses heard God say He would destroy the people of Israel, he pleaded with God. "No, Lord, please do not kill them all. What would the Egyptians say? Here You worked so many miracles to help us escape Egypt. And for what? To kill them out in the desert? No, You would not want the Egyptians to laugh at You. Please forgive the people again, I beg You."

Once again God forgave the people. But they had to pay for being so stubborn. Because they had refused so many times to believe God and trust Him, God said they would never get to set foot in the promised land.

"These people must wander in the wilderness," He said. "All of them will die out here, except for Caleb and Joshua, who believed in Me. Instead of bringing them there within a year, as I could have, for you are close by, the people will wander in the desert for forty years. They will die in the desert, and their children will be the ones to finally settle in the land of milk and honey. That will be their punishment."

When the people heard this, they cried out loud. It was too late, though. God had made up His mind.

Despite God's punishment, the people decided if the land was so close, they should go to it right away. They paid no attention to Moses' warnings. They collected all their weapons, saying, "God will help us win against these other tribes." They had forgotten that God had just said, no, they would not be the ones to drive the tribes away.

Their children would do that.

The people went off to battle, all of them except for Caleb and Joshua, Aaron and Moses. These four men stayed in the camp with the ark.

When the people returned, they had lost. Many men had died in a battle which God had not helped them win.

For the next thirty-eight years the people of Israel would wander from place to place. The Lord did not stop leading them, but He did not lead them straight to the promised land. Their punishment was real. They had to spend the rest of their lives walking in circles, so close to Canaan, but never able to enter it.

A STUBBORN PEOPLE

Moses Loses His Patience

Numbers 20:2-11

Year after year after year went by until finally, nearly forty years had passed since the people had left Egypt. In all that time they went nowhere, slowly. They moved from camp to camp. All the grownups who had left Egypt were very old. Their children had become adults and some even had children of their own. In all that time, though, the people still had not learned to stop complaining.

"Moses, we're thirsty!"

"Moses, it's too hot! Where can we find water?" The cries for water could be heard all around the Israelite camp.

"The people are complaining again," Aaron said to his brother. Moses was very, very old by then. He said nothing. He motioned for Aaron to follow him. Together the two men went to God's tent, which housed the ark, or box containing the Ten Commandments.

Moses called on the Lord, asking where they should find water. The Lord told Moses to take his rod and hit the nearby rocks. Then there would be enough water for everybody.

So Moses took his rod and he and Aaron went to the rocks.

"Why did you lead us out here?" the people yelled at him. They still had not learned that God took care of them.

Then Moses became mad. They were like silly babies, each one of them. "Here, you want water?" he called to them. "We'll give you water!" Moses lost his temper and hit the rocks as hard as he could. Water came gushing out. There was enough water for all the people and their sheep and cattle, donkeys and camels.

But Moses had made a mistake. When Moses gave the water to the people, he did not say the water was from God. He had lost his patience and yelled, "Here, we'll give you water," acting as if the water came from the rocks because he and Aaron had made it gush out. He had not given the credit to God and used the time to teach the people a lesson about how God takes care of them.

Moses and Aaron Are Punished

Numbers 20:12-13, 22-29

God was angry at Moses. He said, "Moses, because you did not tell the people the water was from Me, you will not set foot in the promised land either."

At this, Moses felt his heart break. He had never wanted to lead the people in the first place and now he would never get to enter the promised land.

"Yes, Lord," he said and bowed his head. "Perhaps the land is not the most important thing after all," he thought. But he was not so sure.

Later, when the people of Israel had traveled to the foot of yet another mountain, God told Moses to bring Aaron and Aaron's son up to the top of the mountain. Moses and Aaron did not know what to expect.

God spoke to them there and said because Aaron had been with Moses when Moses lost his temper and made the water come out of the rock, because Aaron had also forgotten to tell the people the water came from God, then Aaron must die.

Moses and Aaron looked at each other. The two brothers had indeed made a terrible mistake when they lost their tempers on that day when the people had wanted water. Aaron was a very old man when he died.

God made Aaron's son the head priest. When Moses and Aaron's son carried Aaron's body down the mountain and the people saw their priest was dead, they were very sad. They tore their clothes and wailed, grieving for a whole month.

They missed Aaron now that he was dead. Yet, when he was alive, they had not paid any attention to him and often ignored his warnings. Now that he was with God, they wanted Aaron back.

Moses was the one who missed Aaron the most, though. Aaron had been Moses' big brother, his helper. Together, he and Aaron had fought off the people and pleaded with God to forgive the people of Israel each time they were bad. When Aaron died, Moses felt as though he had a big empty place inside of him which would never feel right again.

War and Settlement of a Part of Israel

Numbers 21:21-35; Deuteronomy 2:26-3:29

When the forty years of wandering were almost over, most of the people who had been in Egypt were dead. It would soon be time for God to lead their children, now the adults and new leaders of Israel, into the promised land.

As the people of Israel traveled, they passed through other countries belonging to foreign tribes who did not like the people of Israel. They saw all the animals the people of Israel had with them and they thought, "We would like all those sheep and cattle for ourselves." The Israelites were often attacked.

The Lord kept His promise, though, and showed Moses and Joshua how to defeat these enemy tribes. Time and time again the people of Israel won the battles. Until finally, they owned whole cities where the women and children could live while the Israelite men went out and fought war after war, slowly but surely defeating the tribes living near the land God had promised them.

Moses and Joshua were the leaders of the people of Israel. Because Joshua and Caleb had been the only two of the spies, so many years ago, who had told the truth, God said they would be the only ones from the group who had left Egypt to go into the promised land.

Moses told Joshua, "Remember that God is with you. Remember how He has helped us win all these battles."

Then Moses fell onto his knees to pray. He pleaded with the Lord, begging Him to let him see the promised land. Moses remembered that years before God had said no, because Moses had not told the people the water coming from the rock was from God. Moses begged and begged to see the new land.

Finally God told Moses he would see the land before he died. "You will see the land, but you may not set foot in it."

And Moses did not argue. He had finally learned, after so many years of following God,

that it was better to obey. God often had better things planned than even Moses could have imagined.

Balaam Knows Best

Numbers 22:1-22:18

As the Israelites fought many tribes, they came closer to the land by the River Jordan. Everyone they fought against, they defeated. For God had richly blessed Joshua and made him think like a great general.

Eventually the Israelites came near the land

of Moab. The king of Moab was called Balak. He saw how many Israelites there were and already knew they hardly ever lost. He sent for all his wizards and magicians, hoping they could tell him how he should fight the Israelites.

There was one wizard who was better than all the others in Moab. His name was Balaam. The king thought to himself, "If I can get Balaam to say bad things about the Israelites, the bad things will come true and I can defeat them." So he sent for Balaam.

Balaam was from Moab. He was not an Israelite. Yet he had heard there was one God greater than all and he believed in that one God.

Whenever he predicted what would happen he tried to find out what God wanted first.

When he heard Balak wanted to see him because he wanted him to say bad things about the Israelites, Balaam told the king's messengers, "Even if I were to get a houseful of gold, there is no way I could be mean to the Israelites. Don't you know? They are God's chosen people and He is the one who helps them win all their battles. No, I will not lie. This is what God told me to say."

The Talking Donkey

Numbers 22:19-24:25

When the king's messengers told Balak that Balaam stood up for the people of Israel, the king said, "Make him come here."

The messengers returned and Balaam agreed. He got on his donkey and rode to where the king of Moab lived. But on the way, his old, reliable donkey acted strangely. Instead of walking down the road, she ran off into a field.

Balaam hit the donkey. "Come on! You lazy beast, the king is waiting for me." As the donkey reached a certain part of the road, though, she did the same thing again. Again Balaam hit her hard. When he brought her back to the road, she ran away yet a third time.

Then the donkey spoke, "Why do you hit me like this?"

Balaam said, "Why are you suddenly so stubborn?"

"Haven't I always done what you wanted and taken care of you, and we were never harmed?" the donkey asked. Balaam nodded. "Well look then," she said.

Balaam turned to look at the part of the road where the donkey had turned away. The Lord opened his eyes and Balaam saw an angel standing in the middle of the road, holding a sword.

"Why have you hit your donkey three times?" the angel asked. "If it had not been for her, you would have been dead by now. I was all ready to kill you if you had tried to get past me."

Balaam asked what he should do. "Do you want me to turn back?" he asked.

"No," the angel answered. "The Lord wants you to be sure and say just what He tells you to when you see the king of Moab." Balaam agreed.

When Balaam reached the king, the king brought him to three different high places where they could look down on the huge camp of Israel, which stretched for miles.

Balak asked the wizard Balaam to curse Israel and promise they would lose. He asked him three times. But each time Balaam answered, "These are a great people. They are God's chosen people. If God wants them to win, they will."

When Balak heard Balaam say such good things about Israel, he knew there was no way his Moabite soldiers could ever defeat the people of Israel. The Israelites had God on their side.

MOSES INSPIRES GOD'S PEOPLE
How to Teach Children about God

Deuteronomy 6:1-25

God told the people of Israel to spend time with their children in special ways. The Lord did not want the people of Israel ever to forget how God had taken them out of Egypt and rescued them.

"When you are settled in your land," He told them, "remember not to worship any other gods but Me. I am your Lord. Always remember the miracles I have performed for you."

This always remembering was very important. The people did not have God's story written down, like it is now, in the Bible. Instead, they learned the rules of God because Moses had taught it to them. They learned from their leaders.

The children did not go to school then. They were taught by their parents. So it was especially important that the parents told the children all the stories of God.

"As the children get older," God said, "make sure they hear all about how it was in Egypt, and how I saved you."

"Use every chance you get to talk to your children, when you sit down at home and when you go for a walk. You can tell them what happened at any time of day or night, when they go to bed, and when they get up again," God said.

The children of Israel were taught by their parents to always say thank you to God. They learned about all the rules God had given Moses. And they learned how important it was to trust God and believe that He loved them.

Those parents who spend time with their little ones, telling them stories and asking them questions, are blessed by God. One of the most important things a mother and father can do for their children, is teach them who God is.

The Choice of Life or Death

Deuteronomy 29:1-30:20

Moses was 120 years old and knew he would soon die. He called all the people together so he could speak to them one last time.

He called out in a mighty voice, "You have a choice!" The people shook their heads. What could Moses mean? "All of you who want to live, raise your hands!"

The crowd mumbled, "What does he mean?"

"Of course, we want to live!"

"Yes, yes!" they called. With a whoosh, the people raised hundreds of thousands of hands.

"All those who want to die, raise your hands!" Moses called out.

The crowd quickly lowered their hands. A silence fell over them and they waited. No hands were raised. Somewhere in the crowd a baby cried. The people waited to hear what Moses would say.

"Today," he shouted, "you have said you choose life, not death. God wants to make a promise to you. He wants to give you food and water, beautiful land and large flocks. This is life. He wants to give you peace. He will give

you all these things if you obey His laws."

"But if you do things on your own, if you turn proud, if you forget the great things God did to save you from slavery in Egypt, then you will die!" Moses paused.

"No! It will be worse than death. This land will burn and everything will be ruined. People will look at you and say, 'It is a terrible thing which has happened to the people of Israel.' Do you believe me?"

"Yes, Moses, we will obey!" the people shouted back. Moses bowed his head and prayed it would be so. He loved the people very much, even if they had caused him much trouble.

It is a sign of what a good man Moses was that he could still love the people after all the mean things they had said and done against him.

"Lord," he prayed, "please stand by them and send them holy men and women who will remind them that they are Your children."

The Song and Last Days of Moses

Deuteronomy 31:1-34:7

Before Moses died, he wrote a beautiful going-away song for his people, the people of Israel. He knew he was going to a different sort of promised land than Canaan. He was going to be with his best Friend, God.

Moses wrote this song so the people could sing it around their camp and cooking fires. He wanted them to teach it to their children and he wanted the women to hum it whenever they were doing their chores.

Moses' song was all about the love of God. It told how faithful God had been through the years, of His power and might.

When Moses had finished singing, he felt very tired. Moses wanted so badly to see the land he had searched for during the last forty years. He asked God if his time had come.

"Yes," the Lord said, "you can see the land now, but you will not cross into it.

Instead Joshua will lead the people, not you."

So Moses called Joshua to him and said, "You must be very brave and strong. The Lord will never leave you. Only dare to be brave."

God told Moses, "Go up the Mount Nebo and from there you will see the land of Canaan." When Moses reached the top, he looked across the Jordan River, toward the promised land.

Moses stood on that hill for many hours. He stood and stared, his eyes drinking in the sight of God's land. Wild flowers covered the hills of grass and tall trees swayed in the breeze.

Moses said, "Thank You, Lord." In some ways, it was enough just to see the land.

And while Moses was gazing out at the land which would soon belong to his people, he died. He died a strong man, still able to see and think clearly. God buried Moses in a valley near the mountain. Moses was the friend of God.

GOD'S GENERAL
The New Leader

Numbers 27:12-23; Deuteronomy 34:8-12;
Joshua 1:1-18

"Be strong and brave!" That had been the last thing Moses told Joshua. And the first time the Lord spoke to Joshua, after Moses' death, the Lord said three times, "Be strong and brave!"

"Be strong and brave! Joshua, you will bring all these people into Canaan. You will have to fight more wars, but I will help you win," God said. "Be strong and brave, obey My laws, and the Lord your God will be with you wherever you go. Be strong and brave!"

That day when Joshua returned to the camp he had good news from God. The cry went up throughout the huge camp, "Three more days!"

"What?" The people turned from their jobs, the cooking and taking care of their animals.
"What's that?"

"In three more days we will cross the River Jordan and enter the promised land! Three more days!"

The people were so happy they started dancing and hugging each other. The entire camp went crazy with joy. After forty long years of walking through the desert, they would finally get to see the land God had promised to Abraham, Isaac, Jacob, Joseph and all their great-grandfathers so long ago.

God had told Joshua that in three days he could lead the people into the new land. Joshua sent the word around the camp and the people could hardly believe what they heard. When their leaders went to Joshua to find out more, Joshua told them they must all work together to help fight off the enemy tribes in the new land.

"We will do all that you tell us, Joshua," they promised. They were very thankful to God that they would finally enter the promised land. Why, it seemed close enough to touch.

"I Spy the Enemy"

Joshua 2:1-3

Joshua stood before the two men. They were the best of his best soldiers, brave and clever. "I have a secret mission for you," he said.

The two men watched their General Joshua. Their dark eyes danced with excitement. They were especially good at secret missions.

"I want you to sneak into the land ahead of us, sneak into the city of Jericho and find out how strong it is. Find out if the people are ready to fight us, how many soldiers they have, what types of weapons they use, and are they made of bronze or iron? Then come back and tell me. After we cross the River Jordan, your information will help us take the city of Jericho."

The men nodded and looked at each other. It was just the type of mission they liked best.

That afternoon the two spies slipped into the city. It was surrounded by great thick walls. At night the gates were closed tight and guards patrolled the tops of the walls, making sure no one went in or out.

As they were walking down a side alley, a shout went up from one of the many soldiers walking in the crowd. "Hey, who are those two strangers?"

"Those look like Israelites!"

"Stop! Spies! Those two men are spies, stop them!"

The two could hear the crowd rushing after them as they turned first this way, then that, dashing through the narrow streets, trying to find a place to hide.

"In here!" the whispered voice came from nowhere. The men stopped, looked up and saw a woman hanging out of a window above them. "In here," she whispered, pointing to the door below her.

Without a second to lose, Joshua's soldiers opened the door, ran in, and shut it behind them. In less than two minutes they heard the crowd rush on by.

"This way!"

"Catch the spies!"

When it was all quiet, the men looked around. They saw the woman standing on the other side of the room. Her face was covered with a scarf and only her eyes showed. They could tell by the way she was dressed, though, that she was a prostitute. It did not matter. At that moment their lives were in her hands.

"I will hide you," she said. "Follow me."

The Spies Escape

Joshua 2:3-14

The Jericho woman led the Israelite soldiers up to the roof of her house and told them to hide. The soldiers waited and when it became dark they saw there would be no moon in the sky.

They could hear all the night sounds of the city below them. Children cried, someone played the flute while a man sang to the tune. In the other direction they heard the voices of two men arguing.

What the spies did not know was at that very moment, the king of Jericho was giving his soldiers orders to search the city and bring the spies to him. It did not take long before they reached the house of the prostitute who had rescued them.

"Yes," the woman said to the roomful of guards crowding around her. "Yes, they were here. What was I to do? They would have killed me if I had not let them hide. But they have gone. They left just a little while ago and said they were going to try and sneak over the wall and back to their camp."

The soldiers looked at her. "Should we believe her?" they wondered.

"If you hurry, you can still catch them," she

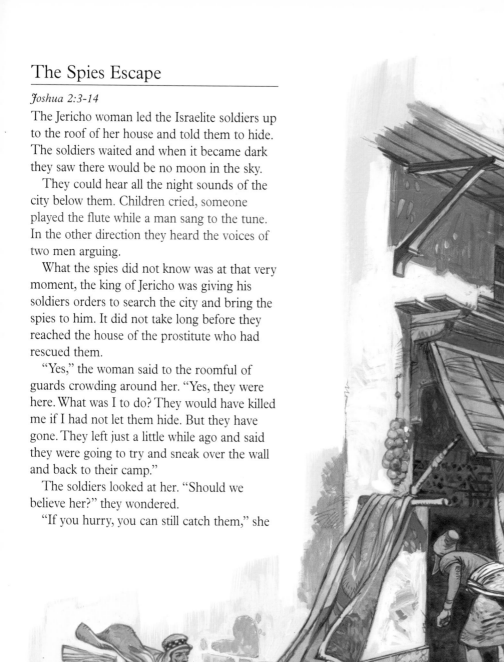

said. She could tell they were not sure of her story.

After another long moment of waiting, the head guard said, "Yes, she's right. After the spies!"

The guards clattered out of the house and rushed out of the gate just before it closed for the night. Now, no matter what, they would not be allowed back in until sunrise the next morning.

"Quickly," the woman called up to the Israelites, "quickly, now is your chance. Hurry and leave while the guards are gone."

The two men climbed out of their hiding place. "I know all about you people of Israel," she said. "God is on your side. He blesses whatever you do. You have won all the wars around here and all the men in Jericho are scared to fight you.

"If I help you escape, will you remember me and my family and not harm us when you take Jericho?"

"Our lives for yours," the men replied. "Yes, we will spare yours if you help us get out of here."

The woman nodded. Then she motioned for them to follow her. And suddenly she disappeared up another set of stairs they had not seen when they first entered the house.

Saved by a Red Cord

Joshua 2:15-22

The men climbed the narrow steps until they found themselves in a tiny room with a low roof. They could barely stand upright without bumping their heads. A small window was the only light.

"Here, this is how you will escape," the woman said. She motioned to the window. When one of the spies went to look out of it, he saw that side of the house was actually part of the wall surrounding Jericho. The woman gave him some rope. "If you climb out here, you will land on the outside of the city. Go into the hills and the guards will not find you. Stay hidden for three days."

The man took the rope from her. "What is your name, woman?"

"I am Rahab," she answered, looking down at the floor.

"Rahab, the only way we can pay you back for helping us escape is if you tie this red rope you have given me to the front of your house. Then when we take Jericho everyone who stays inside your house will be safe."

The other spy came forward. "And," he said in a low growl, "if you tell and we are caught, you can expect no mercy from our army."

She nodded. The men opened the window, stuck their heads out, looked around and fastened the red cord to a pillar. Slowly they lowered themselves out of the house and down the wall, bouncing against it with their feet. When they reached the ground and no alarm was sounded, they disappeared into the darkness. Rahab pulled the rope back inside. She knew it was her ticket to safety. If God wanted the people of Israel to capture Jericho, then they surely would.

On the Edge of the Promised Land

Joshua 2:23-3:13

The spies from Israel hid for three days. When they knew the woman had not betrayed them and they were safe, they ran back to the Israelite camp and reported to Joshua.

"There is no doubt about it, Joshua," the men said. "God has gone before us and struck terror in the hearts of our enemies. This woman who helped us escape said all the men in Jericho were already afraid of us."

"The city is practically ours." Then the three men bowed their heads and thanked God for helping them win their battles. When Joshua was through praying he looked up at his men.

"We will invade Jericho a few days from now. Today, though, is the day for which we have waited so long," he said. At first his officers did not understand what he meant. Then a huge grin stretched across Joshua's bearded face. "Today is the day the Lord will lead us into the promised land!"

The men took up the call and ran to the other leaders throughout the camp to pass on the news. Soon it spread from one end to the other, "Today is the day!"

The people were so excited. They had hoped for and counted down the days, but had been almost afraid it would never come. "Today is the day," they told each other in laughter and shouts of joy.

They were ready. They had packed all their tents and were ready for the final stage of their journey. The river flowed in front of their camp. On the other side of the River Jordan was the land of Canaan, their land. There was God's promised land.

God gave Joshua special instructions for the priests. They were to carry the ark out into the water. But the River Jordan was flooding at that time of the year. All the snow in the hills had melted and so much water poured down the river, it was overflowing. How would the people of Israel ever cross over?

Crossing the River Jordan

Joshua 3:14-4:24

Joshua ordered the priests to carry the ark across the river. The priests looked at the fast-moving waves and shook their heads, but they obeyed. As soon as the priests' toes touched the water, despite the flood, the waves reared back and formed a huge wall, just as the Red Sea had done. A dry path stretched before the priests who carried the ark.

They walked out to the middle of the river, and not a drop touched them. They were perfectly dry! Then Joshua called for the people to follow. Family by family, camel by camel, all the people and donkeys and cattle crossed the River Jordan that day. They walked around the priests who held the ark. The river built up into a gigantic wall as they crossed over.

It took all day for the people of Israel to pass by the priests, into the new land. But when everyone was on the other side, Joshua looked down from the hill where he had been watching everything and remembered the promise of God to his forefather Abraham.

God had said, "I will make you into a great nation, and you will number more than all the stars in the sky and this land of Canaan will belong to you."

There Joshua saw stretching before him countless people, all people of Israel, all members of Abraham's family. And now they had come home. After nearly five hundred years, Abraham's children had come home to the promised land.

Joshua ordered two boys to run back out into the river. They picked up twelve dry stones from the place where the priests stood with the ark. Then the boys and priests stepped away from the spot. As they came up onto the riverbank, all dry and safe, the waters crashed back into place. Then the boys and the priests set up the stones as a reminder of the time and place when God brought His people to Canaan and made the waters of the River Jordan dry up.

Joshua called out in a mighty voice, "This is to remind us and all the people on the earth that our God is mighty and we should always respect and obey Him. See what our God has done? He has brought us home!"

And on the word "home" the people broke into a mighty cheer. At that moment they loved God and wanted to follow God's man Joshua. The people of Israel had come back to the land of Canaan. Their long years of wandering were over.

"Praise God!" they called out.

Reader's Digest Young Families
Old Testament

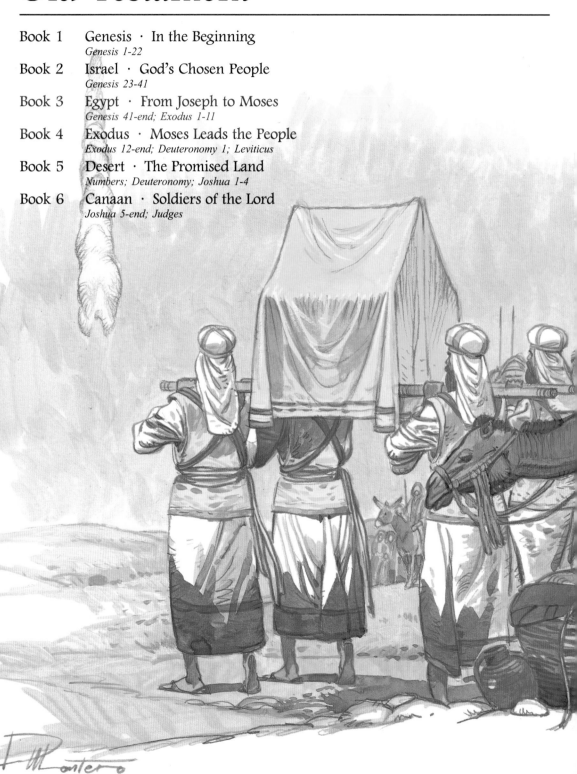